Praise for *David's Chopped Liver*

"In this wise, witty book, David Weisberg invites us into his extraordinary personal journey to donate his liver to an anonymous recipient. The book brims with insight into the power of compassion and courage that lies within all of us, ready to be awakened to improve the state of humanity."

> - Daniel L. Shapiro, Ph.D.
>   Associate Professor of Psychology, Harvard Medical School, and author, *Negotiating the Nonnegotiable*

"David's book reads like a high energy creative project, and the characters play their roles with gusto, including the star of the book, David's Liver! David shares his liver operation song playlist, songs to help foster an environment for healing, and it occurred to me that David's Chopped Liver is perhaps a swatch of a larger patchwork journal: David's Especially Animated and Curious Adventures. In this particular episode, David really truly saves a life!"

> - Alice Ripley
>   Tony Award-winning actress, *Next to Normal*

David's Chopped Liver

My Journey to Become
an Altruistic Living Organ Donor

David Weisberg

David's Chopped Liver
My Journey to Become an Altruistic Living Organ Donor

2020 Paperback Edition, *First Printing*
© 2020 by David Weisberg

ISBN: 9798644106479

CONTENTS

Foreword

Arthur Kurzweil

You have before you a rare and extraordinary book.

The topic at hand seems simple enough: the author decides he wants to donate a part of his liver to someone who needs it.

So, regarding its author, David Weisberg, the one thing we do know is this: he saved a life.

Few people can say that.

Or do it.

Or experience it.

Or write about it.

David Weisberg has done all of this.

Surely the donation of an organ to save a life is a supreme act of generosity. But not surprisingly, in the same spirit of generosity, David Weisberg has taken the time and effort, along with his real gift for writing, to share his profound journey with us.

He shares his questions, his doubts, his moments of elation, his moments of sadness, his laughter, his tears, fears, pain, patience, impatience, love.

Giving someone a gift of a liver, a gift of life, inspires us.

Giving the reader of this book, this celebration of life, an opportunity to come along with its author is also a gift.

David Weisberg, in his own unique way, has written a sacred book.

For what is more sacred than human life?

David Weisberg is a generous man.

Before You Begin But After I've Finished
April 20, 2020

I hate needles.

I had a random memory last night of a day in 8th or 9th grade when our science teacher gave everyone in the class a lancet, asking each of us to do a quick stick into our finger and squeeze a drop of blood onto a slide so that we could look at it under the microscope.

I won't name the teacher, although I'm fairly sure I could; but it's absolutely unfathomable to me, for countless reasons, that such a thing would happen today. I remember kids in my class sticking each other, and one good friend having no qualms running around the room offering to squeeze his blood onto others' slides.

But I simply couldn't do it. And I wouldn't let anyone else do it to me. The whole idea made me squeamish. I was scared.

That aversion wouldn't end in high school. Indeed, it lasts until today.

I share with you the story of my journey to be an altruistic living liver donor in the hope that someone, at least one reader, might be inspired to overcome their own fears – if any – to change (and perhaps save) someone's life.

It wasn't with the intention of publishing a book that I did this writing (perhaps with the exception of the last chapter), but instead to keep my close friends and family fully informed as I went through what for me, as well, was a life-changing process.

My approach to writing was fairly simple – be as transparent as I could possibly be without disrespecting others whose lives in any way intersected with my story. If, at some point, I provide too many details or am slightly too graphic for your tastes, I apologize. My hope was – and is – to provide a full and true picture of the experience – or, at least, *my* experience; the pain and joy, the frustration and exaltation – of being a living organ donor.

Please note that, as these chapters were originally written as a blog, any references to times and circumstances are relative to the dates in which the entries were written and not to the publishing of this book.

I share my story with deep gratitude to so many people who provided support to me along the way, including Elaine Lander, Alison Cole, and Dr. Abhinav Humar at University of Pittsburgh Medical Center (UPMC); Dr. AnnMarie Liapakis and Dr. Sukru Emre at Yale New Haven Hospital; my father, Joel Weisberg; my daughters, Hannah and Alison; and so many close friends who shared with me both their encouragement and their loving concern.

This book is dedicated to the three people who made my journey possible:

- Rabbi Jeffrey Greenberg, whose example as an altruistic living organ donor inspired me to consider doing the same

- My mother, Nancy Weisberg, of blessed memory, in whose honor I chose to donate my liver
- My dear friend, Carol, who shouldered the heavy and difficult burden of seeing me through my surgery and recovery

It's also dedicated to a young boy named Eli whom I had the pleasure of meeting for breakfast six months ago.

Finally, I publish this book not to make myself out to be any kind of hero. I don't consider myself to be one. I was inspired to change someone's life, and I figured out the best way that I could do it.

But I also know that there are countless ways to change and save lives, and there are real heroes who give of themselves on a daily basis in ways so much more than I have. Those heroes, some of them my very close friends, represent what I aspire to be.

As you read, I hope you'll be inspired to consider how you might write your own story.

**What I Probably Won't Be Doing This Summer,
And Why I Still Want to Tell You About It**
May 28, 2018

I'm someone who likes to make big plans and to make those plans far in advance. What that's meant for me in the past couple of years is a lot of travel; and I still have countless destinations and adventures to cross off my list.

But, on the evening of December 8, 2017, I was inspired to begin creating plans for this summer that were different.

As I lay in bed that evening, I had turned 49 just a month earlier. I had within the past couple weeks purchased a ticket to fly to Cambodia in March, with Angkor Wat being the highest place on my bucket list. But, with 50 now firmly in my sights, simply planning another trip didn't seem quite profound enough. My travel adventures have been personally powerful, but I wanted to find something where the power of the journey went beyond me.

It was a series of cascading revelations and circumstances that evening that led me to the decision that I'd begin putting into place the following morning:

1. I was healthier (and am healthier) than I think I've ever been before. I had set a goal last July of losing 49 pounds by my 49th birthday. I had met and surpassed my goal, and, by December, my weight loss was nearing 60 pounds. I was exercising regularly and feeling great (which I still am). And, with some previous changes in

my diet, I was no longer getting sick with nagging coughs that had been part of my life since high school. I wanted to figure out how I might share my good health with someone else.

2. I remembered my friend (and hero) Rabbi Jeffrey Greenberg, who, a number of years ago, saw something on the internet about someone needing a kidney and reached out. Although he did not end up being a match for the person he read about on the internet, he would end up donating a kidney to someone else he didn't know. In his case, the recipient was a neurosurgeon. I have always been in awe of that level of self-sacrifice and generosity.

3. When I went online that evening to see what organs someone can donate as a living organ donor, I learned about living liver donation. I was amazed to learn that one can donate a piece of their liver, and the liver regenerates. My mother, of blessed memory, passed away eight years ago from what, while it started as breast cancer, eventually became fatal liver cancer. I have never felt that I have done something properly monumental to honor the memory of my mother.

4. When I visited Ukraine this past October to visit my family's ancestral village, I wrote a trip blog, which many people read; and, since I returned, I've given nearly a dozen talks about my journey. And, after each talk, without fail someone comes up to me and tells me that they were inspired by my blog or by my talk to consider taking a similar journey to find their roots. If I could similarly write and talk about

this new journey, perhaps I could also inspire others to consider doing as I was (and am) hoping to do.

With these four factors intersecting in my mind, I've never had such an easy decision. I woke up the next morning determined to be a living liver donor, and, I hoped, to bring others along on the journey.

I even thought of a name for a blog – "David's Chopped Liver." What could be a better name for a Jewish professional's blog about their organ donation process? *(While I was going to start writing the blog this past January, I decided to hold off, both to keep privacy about my process and for fear the process might hit a roadblock and not move forward.)*

After consulting with a number of hospital transplant centers, I resolved to enter into the process with Yale New Haven Hospital, both because of its proximity and its reputation.

It was my hope to hold back on sharing anything about this process with my family until after I had an approval and was scheduled for surgery, but I learned during the phone intake conversation with Yale that this was an impossibility.

After an initial phone screening during which I was asked some fairly intrusive and personal questions (and after which it was determined I could move forward in the process), I was informed that the next big step would be two full days of appointments at the hospital, and that it was a requirement that I bring with me to the first day of those appointments the person who would be my donor support person during an eventual surgery. Having no partner in my life at the time (or at this moment), that meant needing to share my plans with my father and with my daughters.

I told everyone during a visit home in December, and my father was quick to raise his hand saying he wanted to be my donor support person. I am incredibly blessed to have this righteous man as my father. The girls were also incredibly supportive of my decision.

In January, I was scheduled for two full days at Yale. These appointments included not only the obvious, such as blood tests, x-rays, MRIs, CT scans, and heart monitoring, but also meetings with a psychiatrist, a psychologist, a social worker, and a pharmacist. I met with the surgeon, and we had an informational meeting to learn about the process. (I had assumed this was laparoscopic surgery, but it's much more. The incision, from belly button all the way around the side, resembles a shark bite.)

Incidentally, of the eight prospective donors present during this first day, I was the only one who was not hoping to give to a specific recipient. There is, indeed, a very small number of altruistic donors (and many, many needed).

I should also note that I don't like having blood drawn and I'm scared to death of MRIs, so this also became a great journey in facing some of my own fears; and it, without hesitation, seemed absolutely worth it every step of the way.

Having my father present on the first day meant the folks at Yale getting a much more thorough family medical history than I could ever have shared, leading to additional testing.

I was told up front that this would be the most thorough physical exam I would ever have, and that only roughly 30% of those who want to be donors are approved. And, indeed, any anomaly revealed during the initial testing would lead to more tests and specialist visits.

Between January and May, I would end up seeing an endocrinologist, a dermatologist, and an infectious disease specialist (following my return from Cambodia). I would have supplemental blood tests and CT scans, and, because of family history and false indicators from my weight loss, I even had a mammogram.

I would also learn during the process that I apparently have an undersized liver. While that liver is just fine for me, the doctors determined that it means I could only be a donor to a pediatric patient (or a very small adult). This didn't at all feel like a setback to me. The possibility that I might not only be able to save a life, but, in particular, the life of a child, felt even more powerful.

Around the same time, I learned that my daughter Alison is expecting her first child – and my first grandchild – this fall. That Alison and I might both bring new life to a child in the same year felt deeply meaningful to me.

After months of process and follow-up, and my anxiously awaiting results, I received word last Monday that I have officially been approved by Yale New Haven Hospital to be a living liver donor. Incredibly, for someone who has never considered myself to be particularly healthy, I was cleared through a battery of detailed testing to meet every standard for clearance.

But the letter came with a bit of an empty feeling, as the combination of two things – my undersized liver limiting the recipient to a child; and my having type AB blood, which is fairly rare and limits the recipient to someone who also has AB blood – results in there not currently being a match on the recipient list who needs a piece of my liver.

While that could change any day, the prospects don't feel great for this summer. (And, with the hospitalization and home recovery time needed for the surgery, the only feasible time for me to have the surgery is in the summer.) I have made it clear to Yale that I absolutely do want to stay on the list, and I would be just as enthusiastic to move forward next summer if a needing recipient emerges.

And so, it seems likely that I won't be able to take (or at least complete) this profound journey this summer. Perhaps it will happen next summer, after I turn 50.

And yet, there are still wonderful things that have happened as a result of the process so far –

1. I discovered that I am incredibly and surprisingly healthy.
2. I've gotten to know an amazing and caring team of doctors and professionals at Yale New Haven Hospital. Their guidance and kindness have been extraordinary.

3. I am cleared to be a living liver donor, and, I pray, I will still have the opportunity to become one.

4. Even though I am not yet going through donation surgery myself, I realized that there is benefit now to sharing the process with you. I do so not because I feel I am deserving of any kind of honor, but, instead, because I hope perhaps my story might inspire someone else to consider being a liver donor as well. I knew so little about the process before December. I didn't even know that one could be a living liver donor; or that the liver amazingly regenerates. I would feel blessed to speak to anyone about the journey.

And, I should be clear, I know that, for countless reasons, being a living organ donor – and particularly an altruistic living liver donor – isn't for everyone. I have a particular set of circumstances – my age, my health, my financial security, my lack of dependents – that make being a living liver donor a very sensible consideration for me. It won't be for everyone.

Many things will still be happening in my life in the coming months. I will become a grandfather in late September or early October. I will turn 50 in November.

And, whether or not I become a living liver donor this year or next year or the year after, I have begun a profound journey this past December. It's a journey that is made more profound because of the impact it will have on the life of a child and the lives of that child's family, and on me.

It may take longer than I anticipated; and it feels worth waiting for. David's chopped liver will yet be served.

What I Probably Will Be Doing This Summer
April 14, 2019

Much has happened in my life since I first (and last) wrote about my intention to be a living liver donor. That was May 28 of last year.

Since then, among many things…

> …I joined a great band called "Exit 43" which has brought me tremendous joy
> …I turned 50
> …I became a *zayde* ("grandfather" in Yiddish) to the beautiful Shoshana
> …My daughter, Alison, got married

And, while little happened in terms of prospects for a liver donation over much of the past 10-plus months, I've remained steadfast in my hope to give a piece of my liver to someone who needs it; and I've waited.

In late January, when I reached one year past the date that I originally began my testing, I made two decisions. With no national database to find liver donation matches, and Yale still not having a match for me (as they had determined, my pool was limited to a pediatric patient with AB blood), I resolved I needed to begin reaching out to other hospitals to see if they had a potential recipient.

And I decided it was time to begin speaking publicly about my process, as part of a talk I would begin giving this spring at local synagogues. If I couldn't donate my own liver, I at least wanted to see if I could inspire others to consider being living organ donors.

My initial outreach to hospitals in the northeast proved to be fairly fruitless. In those few cases that I did hear back (which was upsettingly less than 50 percent of the time), the answer would be "No, we don't have a match for you."

NYU Langone Hospital did ask to see the images of my liver that Yale had taken, but their response ended up being similar to Yale. "Your liver is suitable for a pediatric patient, and we don't have a match."

In late February, I began my synagogue speaking tour, weaving the story of my intended donation process into a longer talk that includes topics ranging from dogs to baseball. The talk was almost always well-received, with an equal amount of folks wanting to talk with me afterwards about my liver as wanted to speak about dogs. (I'm always happy to speak about either topic.)

And something really extraordinary happened. I began to get calls and emails from those who had heard my talk and who wanted to tell me about a news story they heard about a child somewhere in the country who desperately needed a liver or who wanted to refer me to another hospital. (Last week, I had three separate emails about the same child in Wisconsin who is awaiting a liver. He has Type O blood, and I pray they find a match for him.)

It was at my talk at Beit Chaverim Synagogue in Westport that one of my friends, Ivy, who has personal experience as a two-time organ transplant recipient, called me over after I had finished speaking and suggested that I reach out to University of

Pittsburgh Medical Center (UPMC), who she knew to be leaders in the organ transplant field.

I parked that information somewhere in my brain. Pittsburgh isn't as convenient to coastal Connecticut as New York or Boston.

And then, a few weeks ago, I reached out. I received a response fairly quickly from the surgical director of the living donor program at UPMC saying, "I would be happy to review your CT and volume measurements of your liver if you could send me the report of your scan and if possible a CD with the scan itself. We have used many smaller livers in adults with success so that may be an option as we do have some potential adult recipients at the present time. Let me know if you would like to pursue that."

I immediately reached out to Yale to forward a CD of my scan to UPMC.

And again, I waited, as I have been waiting for over a year…

…until Friday, April 5, when I received an email from Erin, the Director of Kidney and Liver Donor Programs at UPMC, reading: "The Dr. reviewed your scan. Will you give me a call when you have a moment?"

I called Erin immediately, and she told me that the surgical director had reviewed my scans and, from his experience, felt that I had more than enough mass to donate my liver to an adult. She asked if I wanted to pursue finding a match at UPMC, and I leaped at the opportunity.

And then, this past Tuesday, April 9, I received an email from Erin reading: "I wanted to let you know that our living donor medical director reviewed our wait-list and was able to find an appropriate recipient for you."

For a moment, I sat in my chair stunned and motionless. While I hadn't given up my desire to be a donor or my belief that there was someone out there whose life I could help save, I had grown doubtful that it would ever happen. In my mind, I had given up hope.

I followed up immediately with Erin and with Elaine, the Living Donor Transplant Coordinator. They told me that they have an adult match to be a recipient for my liver.

While there are still a couple of boxes to check off with pre-surgical testing, the folks at UPMC are so confident about our ability to move forward that we've put a date on the calendar for surgery: Monday, July 8. And so now, the odyssey that I began on December 8, 2017 is finally moving forward. I couldn't be more excited.

There are plenty more details and learnings and stories to happen along this journey. And I hope to take you with me, with the intention to post frequently throughout the process.

David's Chopped Liver will finally be a reality.

Meeting the Team
April 25, 2019

When I received the email on April 9 from the Starzl Transplantation Institute at UPMC in Pittsburgh notifying me that they had a matching recipient for my liver, and when we subsequently scheduled a tentative surgery date for July 8, we were aware that part of that tentativeness was due to my need to meet with the transplant team at UPMC for interviews and testing. While the transplant center was willing to accept many of the results from my process at Yale last year, including the results of CT scans and cardiac stress tests, there were things they wanted - and needed - to do on their own.

And those things happened on Wednesday of this week in Pittsburgh.

While UPMC would typically have a prospective liver donor come in for two days of testing, plus a day of pre-op consultation and testing closer to the surgery date, they were kind enough - understanding the 7-hour drive I live from Pittsburgh - to consolidate all of those things into one day, with an understanding that, if approved for surgery, I will have some blood tests done here at home and sent to Pittsburgh in the weeks before my transplant.

It was a full and exhausting day, beginning with such a volume of blood being drawn from me that I wasn't sure I had much left and the need for a urine sample (for which thankfully much less volume was needed than for the blood), and ending with an EKG and chest x-ray.

But, in between, the heart of my day - as it had been at Yale last year - was spent in meetings with members of the transplant team, including financial services, social work, psychiatry, pharmacy, patient advocacy, and hepatology, all orchestrated by my living donor coordinator, Elaine, who will be my point person at UPMC throughout the process. These meetings are a bit of a two-way interview, as it seems that part of the intent is to inform and give me the opportunity to ask questions about the transplant process while the other purpose is to interview me about everything from my health history (physical, mental, and emotional) to my financial stability to my motivations for wanting to be a living liver donor (which I had to explain at least four times over the course of the day).

The highlight of the day was meeting Dr. Humar, who, if everything goes right, will be my surgeon. Dr. Humar does all liver transplant surgeries at UPMC, an operation he has performed approximately 400 times (possibly more than anyone in the country). We looked at some pretty amazing images of my liver (taken at Yale last year), and Dr. Humar eased some concerns that I had been given about the size and structure of my liver. While the present intent is to take the large lobe of my liver (which should be approximately 60% of my total liver), if it proves that my large lobe is too large a percentage of my total liver, the doctor may choose to take the smaller lobe; but none of that will be known for sure until I'm opened up and he can see directly. He assured me that he would leave me with at least 30% of my liver (which should grow back to a full-sized liver in about two months). Dr. Humar is an impressive person, without a hint of arrogance, and his knowledge and attention to detail put me at ease. And it's particularly exciting to know that he has a specific patient in mind to receive my donation, even if I don't know who that person is.

What also became clear is that it's uncertain that I will ever meet the patient who receives my donation (assuming the process moves forward). While I had already decided that I did not want to meet the recipient prior to surgery, but only afterwards (the reasoning of which I will perhaps explain later), I learned from Elaine that, sometimes the recipient doesn't want to meet the donor at all, and sometimes the donor never knows whether the donation ended up restoring the health of the recipient. I understand that, and it doesn't in any way affect my desire to move forward. While I would love to meet the person who receives my liver, I also recognize that, according to Jewish teaching, anonymous giving is, in fact, a higher level of giving than that of knowing the recipient. What will be most important to me is simply to have done it.

Some random notes from throughout the day:

- I was informed that there is a $50,000 fine if it is discovered that someone accepted payment for donating an organ.
- I learned that, while blood flow to the two lobes of the liver typically comes from one artery that splits into two, I actually have separate delivery to each lobe, which apparently eases part of the surgery. And some of the images of my liver and circulatory system were just spectacular to see.

- The only time I got at all light-headed during the day was when I was being told about the many tubes that would be inserted in me during and after surgery. Some M&Ms helped to cure the light-headedness.
- Some of the little things that UPMC does to show donors they are appreciated were very sweet, from free parking to coupons for the hospital cafeteria.
- I was told that my urine is beautiful. That's not a compliment one hears every day.

Everyone who I met with on Wednesday will be meeting next Tuesday, at which time Elaine will present my case to the team for approval. There's no one I met with today who didn't seem totally confident that things will be moving forward, but final isn't final until it is approved (and then even until the day of surgery).

And so, for now, I wait until next Tuesday afternoon or Wednesday, with the hope of receiving a call telling me that I've been approved as a living liver donor at UPMC. But now I've met the team, and they've met me, and it feels great. And, unlike last year's approval at Yale, this time I'll know that there is a matching recipient waiting; and that makes all the difference in the world.

The Waiting is the Hardest Part
April 30, 2019

The waiting is the hardest part. I've been waiting for about 15 months now to be approved as a living liver donor with a matching recipient.

And after my stalled process when there wasn't a matching recipient for me at Yale, I was poised this afternoon to receive that phone call that I've been waiting for well over a year. This afternoon, I was told, they would be presenting my case to the transplant team at UPMC for my formal approval as a living liver donor, with my surgery already scheduled for early July.

Last week I had been to Pittsburgh for my final tests and met with members of the transplant team. I had my interviews and consultations; and the surgeon, Dr. Humar, and I had a look at some spectacular images of the liver that I am hoping to (at least partially) give away.

There are those calls that I can remember waiting for. In high school, it was a call about the results of a theatre audition. When I got older, it was the call about a job I had interviewed for. As a parent, it was waiting for that call from a teenage daughter who just got her driver's license telling me that she had safely arrived at her destination. (Those calls from my teenagers rarely came, of course, but thankfully they always arrived safely.)

But waiting for this call has felt different, and, over the past couple of days, I've tried to temper my expectations from what I felt near certain would be a "yes."

The first signals came to me on Friday night. Being registered on the UPMC online system, I started getting regular notifications every time one of the results from last week's tests came through. And while, of course, I have no idea what most of those test results mean, I started looking at them. That's at least as dangerous as self-diagnosing on WebMD. I quickly noticed that some of the results were flagged with a signal that looked like an exclamation point within a circle; and as I looked at those results, I could see that some of them appeared to show results outside of typical ranges.

One, for example, clearly showed that I once had chicken pox. (That's true.) Another showed that I apparently once had mononucleosis. (I didn't know that I ever had, but okay.)

Still others related to things I don't quite understand. One had something to do with clotting. Another had something to do with hepatitis (which I for sure don't have).

Granted, I don't understand any of it, but it was enough to make me concerned. I didn't tell anyone why, but I tried my best to temper my expectations. I've seen enough certainties go awry to know that nothing is a certainty.

I learned this morning that the transplant team would be meeting at 3 pm today to discuss my case, and I hoped beyond all hope that I would at least receive a call this afternoon and not have to wait until tomorrow morning.

And then my phone rang at 4:41 pm. It was Elaine, my living donor coordinator.

Elaine asked if I was okay when I answered the phone. Clearly my voice was quaking a bit. I told her that I was fine, just a bit anxious waiting for her call.

Elaine told me that the transplant team had met to review my case…

…and they wanted to talk about it again.

Dr. Humar couldn't be there today because he was in surgery. The hepatologists wanted to discuss the size of my liver, and they couldn't have that conversation without Dr. Humar present. And there is one blood test that they had overlooked, which screens for prostate cancer, that they need me to get done.

While I'm not concerned about the blood test, which I can get done here, once again there is discussion about the size of my liver, not a new topic on this journey. I feel comforted by the conversations I had with Dr. Humar last week when we looked at my images together, but I don't feel as assured as I did yesterday, or even earlier today.

Dr. Humar is scheduled for surgery again next Tuesday (which isn't typical), which means my case may not get discussed again for at least two weeks.

Today I thought I was going to cross one finish line, completing a marathon, and then racing towards a July transplant.

What's another two weeks after 15 months? Just another leg in the journey, I suppose; and two weeks feels like a lifetime.   While I'm just waiting to *give* my liver, I can only imagine how much more difficult it is for someone waiting to *receive* one.

The waiting is the hardest part.

Playing Doctor -or- Patient(s) is a Virtue
May 7, 2019

Tomorrow marks exactly one-and-a-half years since December 8, 2017, the day that I quite spontaneously and decisively decided that I wanted to give someone a piece of my liver. And, while there have been times that I've felt close to the finish line since then, this week I was feeling pretty far away.

Having gotten word last week from Elaine, my UPMC Living Liver Donor Coordinator, that, while I was to be presented to the panel for approval last Tuesday, Dr. Humar, the surgeon, was unable to attend and so my case could not be considered, AND that Dr. Humar would likely be in surgery again this Tuesday, meaning I would have to wait for two weeks, had left me feeling pretty blue.

In the past couple of days, I heard from some friends whose family members were involved in a successful chain kidney transplant over the past few days, and, while that news left me feeling very inspired, those who know me well will understand that it also made me even more impatient. I wanted to do my transplant too.

Patience is not a virtue held strongly by this potential patient. And with nothing to do but wait, I reverted to my worst instincts and started doing that which I warned about last week - playing doctor.

I had gotten a notice that there were additional test results for me online, so I went to take a look. I imagined I'd find the results of the blood test I had taken last week for prostate cancer. Indeed those results were there, and, thankfully, they were clean.

But there also seemed to be another new set of test results, titled *CT 3D Rendering with Postprocess*. I needed to take a look. I opened it up to read "Post processing of the data from CT imaging of the abdomen acquired at OUTSIDE HOSPITAL on 01/26/2018 was performed on an independent workstation under my concurrent supervision for the determination of liver volumes for LIVER DONOR. 3D volume-rendered images were generated, and the volume is recorded below."

It was immediately clear that this was UPMC's independent examination of the images taken at Yale to determine the size and composition of my liver. This, in terms of the decision as to whether my liver is too small or otherwise inappropriate for donation, seemed like the holy grail.

And while I'm not a hepatologist or a liver surgeon (or indeed any kind of doctor), I of course needed to interpret the results. This involved some quick online research for standard liver volumes in adult males and understanding how to convert cc to ml (which is really not a conversion at all). What seemed to be evident to me, but what of course I had no way of absolutely knowing, was that my liver seems to be of a normal size. And, just as importantly, I had been told by Dr. Humar that, while he hoped to take the large lobe of my liver, he would not take the large lobe if it was more than 70% of my liver, meaning we might need to wait to find another matching recipient. By my calculations, the right lobe, which is the large lobe, measured up almost exactly at 60%, what I understand to be the perfect ratio.

So I grew optimistic. While I'd have to wait another week, I at least grew more confident - and granted I could be entirely wrong - that my liver was appropriate for donation. At least that felt better.

And, in touching base with Elaine yesterday, I was given a tiny glimmer of hope that perhaps Dr. Humar might, in fact, end up being at the meeting today.

I checked to see what time I heard from Elaine last week. She had called at 4:41 pm. I wanted to leave work a little early today to try to squeeze in my daily walk/run before heading back for an evening meeting, but I also didn't want to miss Elaine's call.

At 3:27 pm, I emailed Elaine: *Of course, I am curious to know if Dr. Humar was able to attend the meeting this week.*

At 4:17 pm I heard back from her: *No he was not.*

I was a bit disappointed, but not surprised. This is what I expected. This prospective patient would need to be more patient.

I emailed Elaine back: *ok, i guess we are waiting until next tuesday then?*

And I headed home. When I got home, I felt too down to take my walk/run. I made a bowl of popcorn and slumped on the couch. I was exhausted from all of this.

As I was about to finish my popcorn, I checked the email on my phone.

There was another message from Elaine: *Okay so even though Dr Humar was not there, Dr Ganesh came in and presented you. And…you were approved to donate!*

I read the email five or six times. My head almost burst. I did a little dance. While I'm not 100% sure, I think I may have momentarily levitated. I called my loved ones bursting with excitement.

I'm really doing it! I'm really giving someone a piece of my liver!

So What Would My Mom Think?
May 12, 2019

It's Mother's Day, and my recent tradition to remember my mother, Nancy Weisberg (z"l), on Mother's Day has been to make her kugel, which is my favorite food ever and reminds me so much of her. I'll make that kugel today…and I'll be careful. I could eat that kugel for breakfast, lunch, and dinner, and snacks in between. The recipe includes two full cups of sugar. I'll have a couple of pieces and do my best to give the rest away.

That being said, making (and eating a small bit of) that kugel seems secondary on this Mother's Day.

As I've written before, part of my decision to donate my liver specifically was out of my desire to do something monumental to honor my mother. My mom was first diagnosed with breast cancer in 1997, I believe. She'd fight that, and win, eventually being declared free of cancer. But when it reared its head again (as it seemingly often does) many years later, what started as breast cancer had spread to other places, including her liver; and it is my understanding that her direct cause of death, on December 23, 2009, was from liver cancer.

I had a special relationship with my mom. We spoke almost every day. I was an unabashed mama's boy.

While I'm also terribly close to my father (who will be by my side during and after my liver donation surgery), my connection to my mom was different. I'm not sure if that had anything to do with the fact that I didn't meet my father until I was nine months old - as he was stationed in Hue, Vietnam during the war - but I often clung to my mom. And losing her is something I'm not sure I've ever properly come to terms with, although I clearly understand the reality of it nearly ten years later.

And so one of the reasons I am particularly moved by the opportunity to donate my liver is to honor my mother in a way that impacts someone else's life in the way that she impacted mine.

But it's also caused me to ask an important question: "So what would my mom think about this?"

While I am doing this to honor my mom, my interpretation of Jewish law (and granted, I am not a rabbi) is that we cannot honor our parents by dishonoring our parents. That makes what my mother would think important. If she wouldn't have approved, than I would indeed dishonor her in my attempt to honor her.

While I couldn't get inside my mom's head when she was alive, and I certainly cannot now that she's passed, what I *can* do is speak from my experience, and my experience with my mother tells me two things:

> 1. She would have been extremely concerned and worried. She would have spoken to my father about that. She would have learned all that she could about the risks. She would have lost sleep about it. And she never, never would have said a thing to me about all that concern and worry.

<blockquote>
2. I wasn't always an easy child, or, for that matter, an easy adult. I've always marched by the beat of a different drummer. I'm a risk-taker. I like adventure. And, admittedly (but without getting into specifics), I haven't always made the most prudent choices. And, whatever she may have worried about, my mother always supported me 100% of the way, at the end of the day wishing for my fulfillment and happiness.
</blockquote>

And, in the case of working towards being a living liver donor, I don't believe my mother would merely have quietly worried while being outwardly supportive, I genuinely believe that, despite her fears, she would also have been deeply proud - the same fear and pride I'm sure she felt about my father, who was sent to Vietnam when she was six months pregnant.

My mother loved chopped liver, but I never developed a taste for it like my brother did. So today I'll make my mom's kugel, and I'll eat a little. It will fill my belly and swell my heart.

What would my mom have thought? I think most of all she would have thought "You're doing that? For ME? I love you."

I love you, mom.

My Mother's Amazing Noodle Kugel Recipe:

1 lb fine noodles
1 qt milk
1/4 lb butter
2 cups sugar
6 eggs
1/2 lb cottage cheese
2 tsp vanilla
6 oz cream cheese

Cream cheeses and butter, add sugar, beat eggs, gradually blend into cheese mix, add milk and vanilla, then add cooked noodles.

Bake in buttered pan about 90 minutes @350 degrees

America's Team -or- Why I Wouldn't Want to Meet My Recipient Beforehand
May 22, 2019

I write this on a plane flying out of Dallas, where I've just spent the past couple days.

There's one thing I've been raised to know about Dallas since I was a young child. Dallas is the home to the Dallas Cowboys; and, as a Philadelphia Eagles fan, I despise the Dallas Cowboys. The Cowboys are the Eagles' arch-enemy. The whole "America's Team" thing. The reality that for so many years the Cowboys won championships and the Eagles didn't. But two years ago, the Eagles won the Super Bowl for the first time ever. I packed my Eagles Super Bowl Champions t-shirt. I was ready to wear it around Dallas and take a photo with it in front of the Cowboys stadium. (I might even make a rude gesture in the process.)

After going to the stadium for my photo session (and making my rude gesture), I found myself in Boot Barn, a mecca of cowboy boots and Western wear. I saw it as a cultural experience. I had no idea that cowboy hats and boots could be so varied (and expensive for that matter). I thought maybe I'd at least leave with a bandana (which were less varied and certainly less expensive), until I saw a display of t-shirts that - however offensive my Eagles Super Bowl Champions t-shirt might have been to the locals - upset my beliefs and sensibilities to an extent that it was clear that I wouldn't even give the Boot Barn the $2.75 necessary for a bandana purchase.

While some of the t-shirts simply featured the logo of the NRA, the National Rifle Association, an organization that I find unequivocally abhorrent, others featured slogans and graphics such as a picture of a semi-automatic rifle with the text "My Rights Don't End Where Your Feelings Begin." What seemed a fun cultural experience quickly began to turn my stomach. I had to leave the store.

So what does this have to do with my liver donation process?

I've written before about whether I would be interested in meeting my liver transplant recipient.

I made a decision fairly early on in the process that, given the opportunity, I would very much want to meet my recipient after the transplant had taken place but not before.

A few notes on this –

> 1. As I previously wrote, I may never get to meet my recipient, as the recipient may not want to meet me. I understand that, and I accept that I may never have that opportunity.

> 2. I learned during my visit to UPMC that they do not allow donors and recipients to meet in advance for fear that some kind of issue may arise that could affect the donation process. They told me, for example, about a situation in which a donor was to give an organ to a recipient that he knew. A couple of days before the surgery, the spouses of the donor and

recipient got into an argument, and the whole transplant was cancelled.

3. When it was believed that I could only donate my liver to a pediatric patient, I was quite open and interested in having the opportunity to meet that child before the surgery, as I thought it could provide me with incredible inspiration as I prepared for the transplant.

But my general decision that, should I be donating to an adult, I would not want to meet the recipient until after the surgery, has very much to do with my experience on what was otherwise quite a wonderful and enjoyable trip to Dallas.

My thought process was based on the notion "What if I meet my recipient before the surgery, and I don't like him?" What if, I had thought, they take me to meet my recipient, and he's wearing a Dallas Cowboys sweatshirt? Of course, that's a somewhat silly example; but taking my Boot Barn experience into the picture now, what if they take me to meet my recipient and he's wearing that "My Rights Don't End Where Your Feelings Begin" t-shirt with the graphic of the AR-15? Would I feel less inspired about my donation? Would I be wheeled into the operating room with some sense of regret?

Or what if, for example, I discovered that my prospective recipient needed my liver because of a history of alcohol abuse?

The answer for me is that my own politics and convictions are precisely the reason why I would donate to anyone needing my liver to save their life. My belief is that anyone and everyone deserves the right to live. I support the right to free speech, even that speech that I find abhorrent. I believe in universal health care and equality of opportunity. I am vehemently against the death penalty in all circumstances. I believe that everyone deserves an opportunity at redemption. And I believe that substance abuse is a disease.

All this is not to say that if, in a thought experiment, I was given ten different profiles and asked to put them in order from one to ten of whom I would choose to save, I wouldn't be able to do some kind of ranking. It would be dishonest to say that I wouldn't have preferences. I imagine I might choose a relative in need over a stranger, or a child over a senior adult, or a model citizen over a criminal. But I would never want to do that, for fear that my number ten would be the same as others' number ten, perpetually waiting at the end of the line.   And I will feel no less fulfilled, no less impactful, donating my liver to number ten than I would to number one.

A human life is a human life; and, as Jewish wisdom teaches, "Whoever saves one life, it is as if he saved an entire world."

And if I am so blessed to meet my recipient afterwards, I am prepared to feel moved and connected. I will have helped to give someone new life to use as they choose; and I hope my recipient will be inspired to use it for the best - both for him or herself, and for that entire world.

To be clear, I would happily give my liver to a supporter of the NRA, but I would never give a dime to the Boot Barn. And, if my recipient turns out to be a Dallas Cowboys fan, I'll hope that perhaps having a little Eagles-fan liver in him will get him to root for the good guys once in a while.

Like the Spelling Bee, I Was at a Loss for Words
June 5, 2019

It's been two weeks since my last update, and, while it's been my intention to provide an entry every week, to be quite honest I have been at a loss for words. That's unusual for me. It wasn't that I had nothing to say. I just wasn't sure how or what. Last week, they ran out of words at the Scripps National Spelling Bee; and I did too.

For even longer than those two weeks, I've been holding something pretty close to my vest, so much so that I hadn't even shared with it with my daughters and my father for fear of worrying them. Over three weeks ago, the first seeds of doubt - and seemingly much bigger than seeds - were planted that my liver transplant might not be occurring this summer after all.

It was in early May, with my surgery set for July 8, that I decided it would be fun to have a special event on the Saturday night before I departed for Pittsburgh for my surgery. I came up with an idea for a gathering called "A Toast to My Liver," inviting friends to a local restaurant for food and drinks, with a portion of the proceeds to benefit Donate Life CT. I found a local neighborhood restaurant, Hub and Spoke, to agree to be the hosts. I contacted Donate Life CT to help promote the event. My wonderful friend, Jill Sobule, agreed to come up to perform at the gathering. Everything seemed to be moving forward in just the way that I'd hoped and dreamed it would.

In the midst of this planning, some medical professionals I know asked if they could speak to me. I assumed it would be about the event or my getting more involved with the living organ donation advocacy cause.

Instead, these medical professionals, for whom I have great admiration and respect, expressed concerns as to why the various measurements of my liver images, first conducted at Yale and more recently conducted at UPMC, using the exact same images, could have yielded such different results. The measurements at Yale had determined that I could only donate my liver to a pediatric patient. The measurements at UPMC resulted in my being approved to donate to an adult. But did I believe the UPMC results were right simply because I was happier with the outcome? What if the first measurements were correct? What if my liver was indeed too small to give to an adult and the scheduled surgery might put me in some kind of danger?

These medical professionals, whom I consider caring friends and I know were looking out for my safety, asked if they could send my images to a third hospital for independent measurements. It would have been hard to disagree with this sound and prudent advice. I wrote a note with approval to share my images, and, a couple of weeks ago, a disc with my scans was sent to Weill Cornell Medicine.

And I waited, wondering what I would say or do if these third readings reinforced that my liver was too small for an adult donation. What would I say to UPMC? Could they provide information compelling enough that I would still move forward? I was making plans, reserving lodging in Pittsburgh for my family, scheduling this send-off event, arranging my work schedule…and sadly, it was quite possible that it could all be for naught.

Meanwhile, I was speaking to friends, family, co-workers, and more about my surgery, and not saying a thing about an uncertainty that was weighing on me increasingly heavily.

In the midst of all this waiting, and the associated sense of uncertainty, I received a call from Elaine, my Living Donor Coordinator from UPMC. Elaine told me that she had just learned that Dr. Humar, my surgeon, would be out of the country on Monday, July 8, and my surgery would need to be rescheduled. She asked if we could move it back a week to July 15. I agreed, and then Elaine called me again shortly thereafter to inform me that she learned that Dr. Humar would just be returning to the country on July 15 and wouldn't be doing surgery then. I was presented with the options of moving an additional week later to July 22, or a week earlier to July 1. I learned that my father and daughters would be unable to be in Pittsburgh if I scheduled for July 22, which pushed my choices to July 1 or July 29. I worried about July 29 being too late, especially with my hope to return to work in September. I didn't want to be rushing my recovery. I emailed Elaine and ask her to hold July 1 for my surgery. She emailed me back shortly thereafter, apologizing again that Dr. Humar would now not be doing surgery on July 1 but offering me July 5, a date that had never previously been an option. It seemed like a crazy dance.

While I'd have to completely rearrange my lodging, change the date of my "Toast to My Liver" event, and more, I asked her to put me firmly on the schedule for July 5, knowing full well in the back of my mind that I was awaiting results from Cornell that could lead me to cancel the transplant surgery entirely. And I hadn't told my family a thing about it.

But what could I do but move forward, pretending everything was okay?

And so I did; until today, at 11:40 am, when, as I was heading out to a meeting, I received an email:

Thank you for checking in. We have received results from the NYPH team. They are calculating right lobe volume as 64% and left lobe volume as 36%. This makes us feel reassured that you will be safe, and we wish you the best with the donation.

I'm not sure how to describe reading that email. It was almost as if I just got my approval email of May 7 all over again. While I didn't do a dance or levitate this time, I exhaled as long as I can imagine one could exhale. I was left with no breath and a full heart.

It's been a crazy and uncertain few weeks. My surgical date seemed to bob and weave all over the July calendar, as I waited to avoid a punch in the gut regarding my liver size.

Today is June 5. My surgery was moved three days earlier, from July 8 to July 5. What has been a nearly 19 month journey will be complete a month from today.

On July 5, 2019, if everything goes right, someone - I
don't know and may never know who - will be getting
64% of my liver.   I have a lot to say; and, thinking
about a month from today, I'm still a bit speechless.

What Is It I'm Giving Away?
June 13, 2019

Three weeks from tomorrow, I'm scheduled for my liver donation surgery. And while I've thought a lot about the physical parts of the surgery (while somehow insulating myself from the reality that there's going to be some significant pain involved), I realized last week - much to my surprise - that I've thought little about some of the spiritual aspects of the process.

Over the past weekend, a friend asked me, "So what does it feel like that part of your body will be part of someone else? What does the energy feel like that some of your history will be in another person?"

It can be a gift to be asked a question that you don't know the answer to, as it can get you to thinking; and I've spent much of these past few days doing that thinking.

What does it mean that part of me will be part of someone else? I've had my liver for the 50-plus years that make up my entire life. My liver has been around for my moments of tremendous happiness and those of my most intense sadness, my most significant pride and my deepest shame. My liver was there when I held my newborn daughters and granddaughter, when I peed my pants in first grade Hebrew school because I was afraid to ask to go to the bathroom, when I made Mother Teresa laugh, and when I watched my mother take her last breath. There's nothing that I haven't experienced with it. And, unlike losing a tooth or even having one's appendix removed (I still have mine), those body parts go into the trash. My liver will be recycled into someone else.

So what does it mean that someone else will be walking around with a piece of my liver, a piece of me, my history and stories inside them?

I've tried to avoid speaking to other organ donors to learn about their experience. I spoke to my friend, Rabbi Jeffrey Greenberg, early on to learn about the physical realities of his kidney donation, but I've purposely not wanted to hear from him or others about the spiritual aspects of the experience, for fear that my personal experience could be influenced by what I hear. I've wanted my feelings, my reactions, my journey to be a completely organic and personal story.

But facing up to a spiritual question this week that I hadn't considered and didn't know how to answer, I became curious about cultural and religious beliefs about the liver. I did the kind of research that I know how to do. In Wikipedia I trust, and there I learned that there are indeed a diversity of religious conceptions about the liver.

The ancient Greeks told the story of Prometheus being chained to a rock as punishment, where nightly his liver would be pecked out by a vulture, only to regenerate by the next day. (I'm simply amazed that the ancient Greeks knew that the liver regenerated. How is it they knew this in the 8th century and I didn't learn about it until 19 months ago?)

Plato thought that the liver held dark emotions, while in Zulu culture the word for liver is equivalent to courage.

But, of course, I was most drawn to learn what, if anything, Jewish wisdom had to say about the liver, and was surprised to learn that the Talmud says that the liver is the "seat of anger." I am not a Talmud scholar. I am not sure what, if anything, we're supposed to take from that Talmud teaching today.

Accepting it at face value, I asked myself what would be the implications if my liver were the seat of my anger, and I was giving 60-plus percent of my anger to someone else.

The liver performs a wide variety of physical functions, most about which I understand very little. I can't tell you much about the production or purpose of bile. I can't tell you anything about the regulation of glycogen storage. I have absolutely no idea what that means. What I do know, and what I think most folks know foremost about the liver, is that it serves to metabolize alcohol.

I have never been a frequent or regular drinker. There are times I've drunk too much, but that's been pretty rare at any stage of my life. But, even as infrequent as my drinking has been, I decided to give up alcohol entirely when I started this process. I had cut back almost entirely two years ago when I made some changes to my diet that had been suggested to me as a way to help cure chronic acid reflux and coughing (and those changes worked remarkably well), but I eliminated any consumption of alcohol whatsoever when I decided I wanted to give my liver to someone else (and particularly when I thought the recipient might be a child). To be clear, at no point was I told by any transplant center that I needed to stop drinking. For me, it just didn't seem right to be putting alcohol into a liver that I planned to give to someone else.

(Incidentally, I've had a number of people say to me recently about themselves, "No one would want my liver." It's often said with a chuckle. While they're trying to be funny, I find it bothersome on many fronts. I could say much more about that, but I don't want to get off track.)

In the same vein that I've cleared myself, my system, and my liver of alcohol over the past two years, it occurs to me that I've spent at least that amount of time - if not longer - working to clear myself of anger. As with my limited history with alcohol, I've never been one to frequently get angry, but as I've gotten older (and perhaps wiser), I've found anger less and less to be a productive use of my time and energy. I get annoyed. I get bothered. But I rarely get, and certainly don't hold onto, anger, at least in interpersonal relationships. I've done my best to live a life focused on trust, gratitude, and optimism, and I choose to try to give others the benefit of the doubt.

It's not that I'm not angry about anything. I just try to save my anger for those things that upset me the most about our world. I'm angry about intolerance. I'm angry about the undermining of our democratic systems. I'm angry about inequality of opportunity and the destruction of our planet.

So, as I think about that question of what it means that
someone else will be walking around with my liver, I
don't worry so much that my recipient will be
walking around with my history and my stories, as I
believe those exist in my head and in my heart.

And, just as I've cleared my liver of alcohol to
metabolize, I've also cleared it of grievances against
others. It wouldn't seem right to be giving that to
anyone else either.

And if, with my liver, my recipient gets a little bit
angrier about intolerance, about inequality of
opportunity, and about the destruction of our planet,
well…I'm honestly not sure I would mind that at all.

What I'm Afraid of (and What I'm Not)
June 18, 2019

I have a variety of fears - some rational and some quite irrational. I have a nuanced but extreme fear of heights, very specific to situations where I believe my clumsiness could be my downfall. I can't look over the edge of a high terrace. I am petrified to ride on a Ferris wheel or a ski lift. But I've been more than excited to jump off cliffs (as I've done more than once…into water, of course), as then, I'm *supposed* to be falling.

(Some of my more irrational fears are of emery boards and cheap paperback books with newsprint-type paper, but it's probably not helpful or relevant to elaborate on those here.)

My surgery is scheduled for two weeks from Friday, just 17 days away, and early this morning I went to a local lab to get my final blood tests completed, some of which will be processed locally and three vials of blood that had to be overnighted to UPMC so that they can run tests on site.

I don't like having blood drawn. I'm pretty sure it goes back to one time in high school that I had blood taken at a doctor's appointment and ended up passing out while waiting in line to pay my bill. Since then, I've always gotten nervous about blood tests (although I don't believe I've ever passed out again).

And what I fear even more than having blood taken is having to go into a tube for an MRI. I'm incredibly claustrophobic. The sight of the machine itself causes me to panic. Once, when my back was completely out, so much so that I couldn't walk and had to be taken to the hospital in an ambulance, I nevertheless jumped off the gurney when I saw the MRI machine. I've had to figure out a trick, where I have my eyes covered before I'm taken into the room so that I never have to see the machine. It's the only thing that's enabled me to successfully get through an MRI.

Going into this journey nearly 20 months ago, having to get blood tests and MRIs were my biggest fears about the process; and they remain so.

One of the comments that I've received from some friends and family about my impending liver donation is that it makes me brave. I disagree.

Courage is about doing something that frightens you; and, with the exception of blood tests and MRIs, which are now completed, there has never been anything about the idea of having liver donation surgery that frightens me. So I don't think it's correct to call me brave. For my perspective, I think the children I see riding Ferris wheels are brave. Not me.

So perhaps call me naive. Maybe even foolish. But from the moment that I made the decision - rather spontaneously - on December 8, 2017 that I wanted to give someone my liver, I've never had a shred of doubt about that decision. And, in fact, it was my sense of conviction and excitement about the potential to save someone's life that helped me overcome my blood-letting and claustrophobic fears.

And, as each day passes and my surgery gets closer, I haven't felt fear or second thoughts begin to creep in; and I don't expect that they will.

I have often thought and wondered about what I would do if faced with a situation of making an instantaneous decision that involved putting myself at risk to help others. What if I needed to jump into flood waters or run into a burning building to save someone? What if I could help tackle a potential shooter? What if I had to run out into the middle of a busy highway to rescue an injured person? While I pray never to have such a circumstance, I've always hoped that, if faced with one, I would show bravery and self-sacrifice, that the potential to save someone would help me overcome my own fears.

What I'm doing now is clearly different. The act I am undertaking by choice and with much time for potential reconsideration involves placing myself in the hands of experienced professionals, so the risk - although there admittedly is some - feels highly mitigated.

But I also know that, just like grabbing an impulse item while waiting in line at the store, there are certain decisions I would likely make in an instant that I probably wouldn't make with 20 months of analyzing the potential outcomes; and, I suppose, vice-versa.

What I do know is that, 17 days away, I'm not scared whatsoever. I don't feel at all brave. I feel excited. I almost can't wait.

I won't be riding a Ferris wheel. Instead, I'll simply be jumping off a cliff.

The Story I Can't Tell You
June 25, 2019

It's now just 10 days until my liver donation surgery, and the countdown has begun in earnest.

All the details seem to be coming together as I've hoped they would, and I have a call scheduled on Thursday afternoon with Elaine, my Living Liver Donor Coordinator, to review my pre-op instructions.

And, as of just a few days ago, it seemed as though more fortune was shining upon me, as late last week I received an offer on a home that I own and have been trying to sell in the Berkshires. While it absolutely wouldn't be life-saving for me to sell that house, it would be a great turn of events; and it seemed like it was not only happening, but that the settlement could happen in the days leading up to my surgery. The potential buyers had visited the home with their children, and the kids loved it. They had drawn up a sales agreement to be reviewed. Everything was falling into place in the most exciting way; and to have it all happen so quickly was just a dream come true.

And then, on Sunday night, with the confidence that we were moving full speed ahead, I received an email from my realtor that the buyers had a sudden change of heart and had rescinded their offer. I was crestfallen.

I don't know for certain why they changed their minds. I know nothing about them, what they want in a home, and what else might be going on in their lives. I only know that this was going to be a game-changer for me, and as quickly as it had materialized, it had then vanished. Just like with the house itself, there were two stories; and while I spent a little while sulking, I have no idea what was happening on the other end.

It occurred to me in the past couple of days that, while I've been using this blog to tell you my story over the past weeks and months, there's another story to tell, the story of someone waiting just ten more days to receive a liver.

I don't know anything about that person. I don't know the recipient's age or gender. I don't know why the recipient is in need of a transplant or how long he or she has been waiting. I don't know if the recipient has children or grandchildren, and if so, whether those children and grandchildren (or grandchild, in my case) will be at the hospital as mine will be for me. I don't know who will be there at UPMC to support the recipient during the recovery process or who has been by his or her side while waiting. I don't know a backstory that I imagine (like everyone's) must be complex. I've had pictures in my imagination of my recipient, but the reality is that I know nothing.

What I have learned, and what somewhat surprised me, is that the recipient was informed of our match and of the schedule for surgery at roughly the same time that I received notice that I was approved as a donor. That was on May 7. And so, for nearly the same two months that I'll have known I was donating my liver, my recipient will have known that he or she would be receiving one.

I don't know what it was like to receive that news, and whether the recipient rejoiced at hearing it, as I did. I don't know what that wait has been like, but my surprise in learning that the recipient was informed so early is in knowing that realities could change. What if the third opinion that we requested from Cornell had determined that my liver was too small for an adult donation? What if my blood tests last week revealed something problematic? Or what if, like the potential buyers of my home, I - for some reason, for any reason - simply had a sudden change of heart?

While selling that house will be a big deal for me, it won't save my life. What would it feel like for a recipient to learn that their offer had been rescinded?

There's a story I can tell you in my blog, and there's a story I can't tell you. It's a story of someone who has been waiting for a new organ and a new outlook. And in 10 days, a part of my body and piece of my story will become part of theirs.

I'm taking good care of myself these days, making sure I stay healthy and don't catch something like a simple cold that might delay my surgery.

There's another story connected to me. There's a person and likely a family on the other side of this equation relying on me. And, while I may never know that story, I'm focused and determined to do my part to ensure that the other story ends with living…and living happily ever after.

A Note About Notes
June 30, 2019

It's Sunday night, and the end of the final weekend before my surgery.

It was a weekend filled with one of the things I love most: music. It started early, on Thursday night, at my Federation's Disco Night event, when I got up on stage to sing "Copacabana," which happens to be my least favorite Barry Manilow song (and, yes, I do have favorite ones). It continued on Friday night, when I got to join my band, Exit 43, for a really fun late-night gig at a local bar. Saturday night was particularly special, as two of my most beloved and talented songwriting friends, Jill Sobule and Pete Nelson, came in to perform at my A Toast to My Liver event to raise some support and visibility for Donate Life CT, with Jill playing a special liver-donation version of her hit song, "I Kissed a Girl" (the original song of that name, as opposed to the horrible Katy Perry ripoff song). And it concluded on Sunday with a trip to one of my favorite places to hear music, Tanglewood.

Today was also my first day of prep for my surgery, as I began the daily regimen of washing myself down with a special chlorhexidine gluconate cleaning solution, aimed at preventing infection during surgery. I'll be doing that every day until my surgery. And I've started thinking about packing - not only about taking the obvious things such as clothes and toiletries, but also thinking about those things that I want in my room for comfort. That includes one of my many, many turtle figurines. I put together a collage frame with pictures of my loved ones to sit by my hospital bed. I picked out a *siddur*, a Jewish prayer book, and friends have been giving me other books to read during my recovery.

But it also occurred to me that I ought to think about that comfort I get from that thing I love so much, music. I'm a bit old-school, still listening to music on a chunky iPod classic, and I thought it would be helpful to put together a special playlist for those moments when I'm looking for comfort during my recovery. I scanned my fairly massive iTunes library and put together a list. That list doesn't include every artist and every type of music I love, as I was seeking those tunes that more generally give me a sense of calm. So while I enjoy some heavy metal and punk, you won't find "Flying High Again" or "Moon Over Marin" on this playlist. Instead, the songs include some by my favorite songwriters and friends, with many of those being one and the same. The list includes songs that remind me of special people and times in my life. And it includes songs that simply give me a sense of peace and warmth.

I still have a few days to refine my liver playlist, and I'm sure that I'll have moments in the coming days where I'll say "Oh wait a second, what about *that* one?" But I'm feeling happy with my progress, as considering how I can help take care of myself and create the right environment for recovery gives me a sense of greater control as I enter into what I know, despite my excitement about the process, will be some challenging times this coming weekend (and beyond).

I'm happy to share my list with you here.

<u>My Liver Playlist</u> (as of 6/30/19)

A Case of You - Joni Mitchell
A Heart Needs a Home - Richard & Linda Thompson
Accidentally Like A Martyr - Warren Zevon
After the Party's Over - Pete Nelson
Albuquerque Lullaby - Dan Bern
Alison - Elvis Costello & The Attractions
All Good Gifts - by Stephen Schwartz, from *Godspell*
America - Simon & Garfunkel
Beeswing - Richard Thompson
Bird in a Cage - Tony Bird
Blues Run the Game - Jackson C. Frank
Bridge of Cherokee - Iain Matthews
Buckingham - Mandy Patinkin
Cactus Tree - Joni Mitchell
Comes a Time - Neil Young & Crazy Horse
Crazy Fingers - Grateful Dead
Dear Amelia - Vance Gilbert
Feed the Birds - from *Mary Poppins*
Flying Home - by Jason Robert Brown, from *Songs for a New World*
Fotheringay - Fairport Convention
Gentle Arms of Eden - Dave Carter and
Tracy Grammer
Get Up Clara - Richard Shindell
Give Me Love - George Harrison
God Only Knows - The Beach Boys
Green and Gray - Nickel Creek
Happy Good Morning Blues - Bruce Cockburn
Happy Little World - Chuck Brodsky
Here Comes the Sun - The Beatles
Hold On - from *The Secret Garden*, performed by Alison Weisberg
Holiday - Michael Hedges
Houdini's Box - Jill Sobule

I'm Comin' Home - Robert Earl Keen
I'm Not Afraid of Anything - by Jason Robert
    Brown, from *Songs for a New World*
Icarus - Martin Simpson
In My Life - Tuck & Patti
Is This Love - Bob Marley & the Wailers
Jetpack - Jill Sobule
Just Like Christopher Columbus - The Nields
Just the Way It Was - Vance Gilbert
Kentucky Avenue - Tom Waits
Leader of the Band - Dan Fogelberg
Look Up - Mark Erelli
Looks Like Rain - Bob Weir
Love at the Five and Dime - Nanci Griffith
Love Song - Bruce Cockburn
Magnificent (She Says) - Elbow
Malibu - Todd Young & His Rock Band
Melinda - Jason Robert Brown
Mercy of the Fallen - Dar Williams
Met Her on a Plane - Iain Matthews
Mother Nature's Son - The Beatles
Navajo - Ben Kaplan
On the Other Side - Janis Ian
One Day Like This - Elbow
Only Wondering Where You Are - Mark Erelli
Overchewer - Anthony Newley
Pick-Axe Love Song - Deb Pasternak
Road to Hell II (Live) - by Anais Mitchell,
    from *Hadestown*
Royal Blues - Rachel Bissex
Shipbuilding - Elvis Costello & The Attractions
Somebody to Love - Queen
Someone to Fall Back On - Jason Robert Brown
Sometimes It Snows in April - Prince & the Revolution
Spark of Creation - from *Children of Eden* by Stephen
Schwartz, performed by Hannah Weisberg
Starry Eyes - Roky Erickson

Superwoman - Stevie Wonder
Telephone Line - Electric Light Orchestra
Terrapin Station - Grateful Dead
The Great Unknown - Dar Williams
The Lighthouse's Tale - Nickel Creek
The Luckiest - Ben Folds
The Sweetest Punch - Burt Bacharach/Elvis Costello
The Wind - Cat Stevens
Time After Time - Tuck & Patti
Together Forever - by Jeremiah Downes, performed
    by Alison Weisberg
Transit - Richard Shindell
True Colors - Cyndi Lauper
Two of Us - The Beatles
Vienna - Billy Joel
Wasteland - Dan Bern
Way to Go on Dreaming - Pete Nelson
Wichita Lineman - Glen Campbell
Wild Horses - The Rolling Stones
Yihye Tov - David Broza
Your Song - Elton John

A Surreal Sign-Off
July 4, 2019

I'm writing from Pittsburgh. We arrived this evening
after a long drive from Connecticut, and tomorrow
morning, at 5:30 am, I am to report to the hospital. In
fact, it occurs to me that, by the time many of you read
this, I will likely already be in the middle of my
surgery.

Clearly, this will be my last blog entry before my
operation. I certainly plan to write more afterwards,
but it occurred to me today that I have enough to say
now for a half-dozen entries. And so, while I get
ready to drink my required Gatorade for the evening
(oddly enough, I believe it's the first time I've ever
drunk Gatorade), I'll share a bunch of thoughts with
you.

MY FEELINGS THIS WEEK AND TONIGHT: While
I am still not a bit scared or anxious about my surgery,
this past week, everything seemed to feel a bit
surreal. The best comparison I could think of is when
I'm going to be traveling somewhere interesting and
exotic that I've never been before (like when I went to
Angkor Wat last year), and it's hard for me to picture
that I'll actually be there the next day, although this is
clearly something very different from that. It feels
surreal because I decided to donate my liver nearly 20
months ago, and, while it seemed for a while that it
might never happen, it's actually going to happen
tomorrow. It feels surreal because, while I've had
surgery before, I've gone to the hospital for surgery
because there was something wrong with me that
needed to be fixed; but tomorrow morning, I'll be

going in for surgery feeling great and, at age 50, in possibly the healthiest shape I've been in my entire life. It feels surreal because it's hard to imagine that tomorrow they will be cutting me open, removing two-thirds of one of my major organs, and putting it into someone else. It feels surreal because I've been spending a lot of time this week thinking about what must be going on in the recipient's mind, what kind of anticipation he or she must be having, and I have no idea. It feels surreal because, for lack of a better way to put it, tomorrow I will very likely save someone's life, someone I don't know whatsoever. I know it's all going to happen tomorrow, but it still seems hard to imagine.

MY WEIGHT: I had a goal of going into surgery at my ideal weight, which I believe to be somewhere just under 175 pounds, the place I reached with my 60-pound weight loss that began almost two years ago. That seemed unattainable just a few days ago, as I found myself one night at about 182 (and quite upset about that); but somehow, magically, I stepped on the scale this morning to see it come up at 174.6. I was thrilled. I won't be weighing myself again before surgery, as I'm not at home with my scale, and because, knowing that I couldn't have solid food after 5 pm today and probably won't for some time, I allowed myself to be a bit of a glutton today (what I like to call a *chazzer* in Yiddish). Knowing that most restaurants would be closed today for the 4th of July, I went out yesterday and picked up a corned beef-and-pastrami hoagie and a side of coleslaw for the ride. I haven't eaten a hoagie like that for nearly two years. And, by the way, so that you better understand my neurosis about my weight, after I weighed myself this morning, I then stepped on the scale again holding the hoagie and coleslaw to see how much weight I'd be adding. They weighed about 1.5 pounds. That's roughly the same weight I've estimated for the two-thirds of my liver that will be removed tomorrow. Even- steven. And the hoagie was absolutely delicious.

AT OUR HIGHEST, WE ARE REMINDED THAT WE ARE STILL HUMAN: While it's tempting to feel like a superhero flying high at a moment like this, I had a reminder this week that, as much time and effort as it has taken to work with great intention to do a good deed for someone I don't know, it can be painfully easy, without intention and often unknowingly, to hurt someone we do know. Without going into detail, my spirit sank, and I was quickly brought back to earth. I think it's an important reminder that, no matter how powerful we might feel in any given moment, we need to be ever mindful that we are flawed and that we are human. My prayer is that we should all be judged by those good deeds we do with great intention and not by those hurtful things we do unintentionally and unknowingly.

ONE OF THE THINGS I'VE BEEN WONDERING:
I've been wondering if I'll dream at all during the surgery. I don't remember from previous surgeries, but I'm anxious to find out, and whether there might be anything special that happens in a dream at the moment my liver is removed (or, even more amazing, when it's put into someone else). I doubt it, but I hope.

MY SUPPORT SYSTEM: Some people have asked about my support system after surgery. In that regard, rest assured that I am blessed. I'll have a total of six people who will be at the hospital for me at various times. Four of those have been with me throughout the process and have always been incredibly supportive of me in this effort. My dad was the first to raise his hand to be my donor support person, joining me for my very first appointments at Yale in January 2018. He is flying up tomorrow from Florida and will be with me through my trip home. My wonderful daughters, Hannah and Alison, and my fantastic son-in-law, Gary, are coming tomorrow from Philadelphia and staying through the weekend.

Of the two I didn't know at the start of the process, one of those is my sweet granddaughter, Shoshana, who will turn nine months old tomorrow. (As I say, that's the day that Shoshana will have been on the outside for as long as she was on the inside.) When I decided I wanted to be a liver donor, I had no idea that I'd become a grandfather (a *zayde*, in my case) by the time my donation occurred. Shoshana's job is to bring me smiles, and I have no doubt that she'll be up to the task. That leaves one more person. On a first date, nearly six months ago, I told the woman that I had connected with online and was meeting for the very first time that what I was looking for in a partner was someone who would be holding my hand when I woke up from liver donation surgery. (You might understand now why I didn't have a lot of second dates.) Amazingly, she is here now by my side. My dear, sweet, kind, patient, beautiful Carol has been there for me since that first dinner, supporting, caring for, and grounding me. She accompanied me on my first trip to UPMC in April. And she drove with me to Pittsburgh today, will be holding my hand when I wake up from surgery, and will be with me through our trip home (and, I pray, after). She is more than I deserve, and I am so very grateful.

MY HEBREW NAME: For those who want to include me in a prayer for healing, my Hebrew name is Chaim Dovid ben Fruma Nehama. I love that my mother's name will be part of the prayer, as so much of my inspiration to donate my liver is in her honor and memory. I ask you, just as importantly, to pray for my recipient as well.

The next time I write you will be on the other side of my surgery. I was thinking today on our long drive about the acceptance speech that actor Andre De Shields gave last month when accepting his Tony Award for his magnificent performance in *Hadestown*, a show that I love. In his speech, he offered three tips:

*1. Surround yourself with people whose eyes light up
when they see you coming.
2. Slowly is the fastest way to get to where you want to be.
3. The top of one mountain is the bottom of the next, so
keep climbing.*

Indeed, in my support team, and in some other dear and loving friends who have been with me on this journey, I have surrounded myself with people who bring me light and love.

It's taken nearly 20 months to reach my goal of being a living liver donor, but it's finally gotten me where I want to be; and, in the moment, it suddenly feels really fast.

And, while I'm finishing one journey, I can only imagine that I - and my recipient - will have new journeys to begin tomorrow.

See you on the other side, having given away something and gained so much more.

Post-Op Pleasure and Pain
July 6, 2019

I'm reminded as I start to write tonight about the disclaimer that some folks have at the end of emails that they write on their cell phone, such as "This email was written on an iPhone. Please excuse any inadvertent errors." Well…this was written by someone who had two-thirds of his liver removed about 30 hours ago and is on all kinds of medication. While I know that medicinally-affected art has produced some of the greatest works in history, I won't be staking such a claim tonight. Still I felt the desire (and need) to write something.

So I had the nurses come in and help me move from my hospital bed to a chair, which, in and of itself, is one of the big steps forward today.

But let me start by saying a little bit about yesterday, the day of my surgery. While I set my alarm to wake me up at 4 am, I'm not sure I even needed the alarm. I woke up on my own. I drank 16 ounces of horrible Gatorade as required, and by 5:15 am, Carol and I were at the hospital, and I was ready to roll. It was all smooth and simple, and, after nearly 20 months of waiting, I was ready to go.

The process couldn't have been easier. Checking in. Getting a bracelet. Changing into a gown. Giving Carol the precious ring that I wear always (and that was given to me by my Bubbie Rose for my bar mitzvah, crafted from my Zayde Harry's wedding band and my mother's engagement ring) for Carol to wear until I was ready to have it again. I had the chance to settle in by listening to a few songs on my liver playlist that I had made for my iPod, and before long, we were ready to meet with the anesthesiologists and get the process started. Dr. Humar, my surgeon, saw me that morning at something like 7:00 am. He said he was going to see if they could use my small lobe (about one-third of my liver) instead of the large lobe, but he wouldn't know for sure until he could actually see my liver in front of him. That felt pretty real.

I remember some process afterwards with the anesthesiologists. I remember that they had told me that I would be awake for two needles going in me - one in my arm and one in my back. But, for the life of me, I can't tell you that I was awake for a needle going into my back.

Instead, I recall being awakened later, asking when my surgery would start, and being told that it was already finished. I was dumbfounded. I was in absolutely no pain. I couldn't believe that I'd actually had any kind of surgery, let alone a six-hour procedure to remove two-thirds of a major organ. In my dazed consciousness, it almost felt like someone was pulling a joke on me, that it hadn't really happened; but, of course, it had.

And I woke up later to be surrounded by Carol and my father, and later by Alison and Gary and the nine-month-old Shoshana. (I didn't get see to my Hannah until today.)

While I'm not sure how profound I can be in the state in which I am now writing, I do want to share some things:

1. I am so incredibly impressed by UPMC and the system here. Everyone is professional and friendly. Things happen on time, and organ donors are treated with incredible respect. I think, despite the long journey, I ended up in the place and with the support system that were meant to be.

2. I'm amazed at how little pain I felt yesterday in the hours following my surgery. It's not even a question of how much. Yesterday I felt no pain, which brings me to tell you about a drug so powerful and beautiful, when used appropriately in a situation properly monitored by medical professionals.

3. Ketamine was, for me, a miracle. Ketamine gave me a pain-free day. And on top of that - and this is coming from a lifelong fan of the Grateful Dead who has never, never, ever experimented in any way whatsoever with illegal drugs - Ketamine gave me the most spectacular hallucinations I could imagine. As I was trying to go to sleep, if I opened my eyes I would see my hospital room, but, when I closed my eyes, instead of getting dark, I was transported to a new and beautiful space, and that space changed each time I closed my eyes. In a highly controlled and safe setting, it felt pretty extraordinary. And this morning, I had other strange physical sensations, such as feeling like I was sitting up or curling up, when in fact, I was just lying on my back. I would have

to use mindfulness techniques to reorient myself to the reality that I was lying flat. Bizarre, crazy, and so interesting. And, once again, I would never condone using Ketamine outside of its prescribed setting; but on a night when I could really use some kind of peaceful escape, abracadabra.

4. I'm progressing faster than I imagined I would. Today they had me sitting up in a chair. I even walked up and down the hall with the assistance of a walker. And I moved out of intensive care into a transplant patient unit, which has made me feel much more like a human being. With all that being said, I would never have imagined how incredibly weak I still do feel. And I was able to quickly bond with my new nurse, Alison, who spells her name just like my daughter, Alison, and is a fellow Grateful Dead fan. While I haven't started eating solid food yet, I did manage some raspberry water ice and to force myself to drink some Ensure, and I was able to keep everything down. I have a suspicion they may try to get me started again on some solid foods tomorrow, as my digestive system adjusts to its new situation.

5. I think it's quite likely that I'll get to meet my recipient in the next few days. Carol and my Dad are convinced that they've seen the recipient and know who it is. Dr. Humar said that he believes the recipient will be open to meeting, but they want to give him some time, as the surgery is harder on the recipient than it is on the donor. While I already feel great about this whole process, I'd be so absolutely delighted to see and meet my liver's new owner.

6. I love seeing the fun relationship that's developing between Carol and my father, who didn't meet until I was under anesthesia.

7. For the first time since the surgery, this afternoon I began to experience some real pain, which of course I expected and is part of the healing process. Alison (the nurse, not the daughter) had told be to let her know if the pain jumped from a 3-4 level to a 5-6 level, which is when she said they would want to intervene. That indeed happened quite quickly, but through a combination of mindfulness techniques and modern medicine, we were able to get things pretty much under control.

Most importantly - and perhaps I should have stated this more emphatically at the beginning of this entry - I DID IT! I gave someone two-thirds of my liver (Dr. Humar discovered that my small lobe simply wasn't going to work), and Dr. Humar told me that, when they attached my liver into the recipient, it started functioning and producing bile right away! That is simply amazing. And, despite the pain I've had today and the interesting hallucinations and the less-than-desirable AirBNB at which I have my family staying, these last couple of days have been pretty extraordinary and magical, the perfect intersection between cosmic goodness and beautiful science, the crossroads of God and humanity, and that's a pretty special place to be living in.

And just a note about Dr. Humar. While I first saw him yesterday at around 7:00 am, I know he was still at the hospital helping with the implant of the liver into the recipient, which probably didn't finish until around 8:00 pm. That's staggering to me. And I'm sure it's just one of the reasons that he seems to be a beloved figure here. He certainly ranks high on my list. (And he finally shared with me that great photo that he took of the piece of liver that they left in me. While I can be squeamish, it really was beautiful to see.)

I'll have more to update in the coming days (including possibly about meeting my recipient) and I'm sure I forgot countless important things in the foggy mystery of the 30 hours since my surgery ended, but I think for now, I need to yield to the forces of pain and pharmaceuticals that surround me. While I can't imagine this entry will be my *Sgt. Pepper's*, I hope it proves worthwhile. As the Sergeant himself would say, "You're such a lovely audience."

This entry was written by someone who just yesterday had two-thirds of his liver removed and placed in the body of someone he doesn't know; and feels fantastic about it. Please excuse any inadvertent errors.

And Then This Happened
July 9, 2019

Many of you who have been following the story of my
liver donation from the beginning may recall that one
of the primary reasons I decided to donate my liver
was to honor my mother, Nancy, who passed away in
December 2009 at age 68 from what was eventually
liver cancer. I was incredibly close to my mom, truly
and unapologetically a mama's boy. I felt like I had
never done anything monumental to honor my
mother, and this was the opportunity to do so.

A number of people have asked me in the past few
days, since my surgery, whether my mother has
shown up in my story. The most obvious question is
whether I saw her during my spectacular Ketamine-
induced hallucinations on Friday night after my
surgery. But, as much as I would have loved that, I
disappointingly didn't.

I would say, and I believed, however, that I was
certain that my mother was with me.

There's a lot I could write about what's happened
since I last wrote a blog entry on Saturday. My
recovery has been remarkably quick. I received great
strength from some songs on my liver playlist that led
to the reactivation of some of my key bodily systems,
most specifically from the wonderful Grateful Dead
lyric, "Let my inspiration flow." There are some
pretty interesting stories about having countless tubes
and needles removed from me, particularly the young
Turkish doctor who told me that in order to remove
the long needle from my jugular vein, I would need

to take a deep breath, then hum, and then she would choke me for five minutes. It turns out that wasn't a joke.

I was discharged from the hospital today, will get a check-up on Friday, and we'll hopefully be able to drive back to Connecticut on Saturday.

Those are minor details at this point, because at around 11 this morning, one of the staff came into my room and said, "Okay, do you want to meet your recipient now?" I had been trying to prepare myself mentally and emotionally for this moment, which I still wasn't sure would actually happen.

Of course, I jumped out of my bed, walking down the hall, all the way reminding myself of those things that, if I had the chance, I'd like to learn about my recipient and those things I didn't. What was clear to me was that I didn't want to know what my recipient was dying from, I wanted to know what he was living for.

And then we went into the room to find a smiling, appreciative man sitting in a chair. I told him my name is David. He told me his name is Joe. He's 69 years old. He was previously scheduled to get a transplant in April and that one couldn't go forward. He has children and grandchildren and he wants to be alive for another couple of decades to spend time with them and see them grow up.

And he told me that he really doesn't like to receive, he likes to give, and that he was inspired by my generosity towards him to figure out what he could do for others. I told Joe that, while I said from the beginning that I didn't care who received my liver, I was so glad that it was him.

It was an incredibly powerful moment. My dad was crying. Carol was crying. I wasn't. I have always bemoaned that I don't cry at the times that I should but always cry at times that aren't necessary. I can't watch the end of an Eagles Super Bowl video without crying, but I don't cry at funerals (including my mom's). I don't quite understand that about myself. It didn't make the moment any less powerful. It's just me.

Joe lives near Pittsburgh but said he and his family will be in New York next year, and he'd love to meet. I told him I'd be delighted to do that, as long as he understood that he didn't need to buy me lunch because he didn't owe me anything. We said we'd say hi again before we checked out, and I walked back to my room.

Carol, my dad, and I talked about how much we liked Joe and what a great moment it was. And it was; just really lovely and quite powerful. And then we went back to talking about other things, like the struggle we were having to find a rental car for my father.

In the midst of that, about 30 minutes later, a lovely, smiling woman walked in our room.

She said, "I just wanted to introduce myself and say thank you. I'm Joe's wife. My name is Nancy."

I shuddered for a moment. I said "I know it's not a proper question to ask, but how old are you?" She responded that she was 69.

I said "All the time through this story, people have been asking if I've seen my mother. And now she's here, in you." I told her that my mother's name was Nancy, and that she passed away when she was 68 and that I had gone through this process to honor her memory.

Nancy said, "Oh, on the day of the surgery, I was 68. I didn't turn 69 until the day after."

I looked at the photo of my mother and me that I had in my hospital room.

And I cried.

I went through this process to save someone's life and to honor my mother; and there she was at the end, waiting to give me a hug and thank me for what I had done.

While I will certainly write more about this journey, I couldn't imagine a more perfect bookend to it.

Nancy and Nancy, this tear is for you.

Re-entry, Reactivation, and Reflection
July 12, 2019

As I write this, it was a week ago at this time that I was beginning to wake up out of the fog of my liver donation surgery.

One of the things that feels most remarkable about the past few days is just how unremarkable they have been. I was discharged from UPMC on Tuesday and returned to this very strange (and unfortunately destined-for-a-bad-review) AirBNB that we rented in Squirrel Hill. One doesn't leave the hospital after surgery expecting to be free of pain; and that's certainly not been the case for me. I've been sore; but most of all, I've simply been exhausted. Walking the stairs or, in particular, digesting a small meal, can seem to take all the energy I can muster, and I find myself quickly sitting back down into a chair or lying in bed. But, all that being said, it's just one week since I had two-thirds of a major organ removed that my body is giving energy towards regenerating at the same time that it's adjusting to it currently not being there in its full capacity.

I was also reminded that I need to be more cognizant of my more limited capacity for digestion, perhaps more so because of the removal of my gallbladder (which happened at the same time they removed most of my liver, simply because my gallbladder was in the way). The post-gallbladder diet is fairly limiting; and, in addition to those things that come up on any google search - no fatty meats, no fried foods, no dairy, no processed foods - I was also told to avoid some of my "go to" foods, such as salad and broccoli and cereals. With that being said, we thought that being back at the house needed to be a time to celebrate, and we decided to order from a local Taiwanese restaurant that Carol, my father, and Hannah had loved. I looked for the blandest thing on the menu and ordered very boring chicken lo mein.

An hour or so later, we found ourselves calling the liver transplant unit and being directed to report to the ER, as I was dealing with significant abdominal pain and a low fever. They tested me, things looked fairly clean, and they sent us back home. (It turns out the low-grade fever was unrelated to the abdominal pain and is now being treated with an antibiotic, which Dr. Humar called in from a conference in Italy.)

Speaking of food, I should note that, while I had been quite determined to go to the hospital for my surgery at my ideal weight (around 174 or 175 pounds), I was shocked in the days following the surgery, when they had me step onto the scale, to see a weight of approximately 192 pounds. I said, "You know I came here to give my liver, not for you to give me a 15-pound weight gain?" They assured me that this was typical, the results of all the fluids pumped into me during and after surgery. Still, I was frustrated and have been feeling a bit bloated.

But other than that, this has been a time for rest, re-entry, and reactivation of my bodily systems, which seem to finally be back in full function.

This morning, I was scheduled for a final early-morning checkup to get the clearance to drive home. While the most important aspect of that appointment, obviously, was to find out if they felt comfortable with our taking the seven-hour drive home, I was relieved when they had me step onto the scale to learn that my weight was already down to 180 pounds. And to my delight, every other measure and check seemed to be ideal, from my vital signs to the healing of my incision, which is going to leave a pretty cool-looking scar. The doctors gave us the okay to head home, which we'll do tomorrow, and I don't need to be back at UPMC for a check-up for four months, at which point they will do a CT scan to make sure my liver has regenerated to its full capacity.

Knowing that we would be leaving tomorrow, there was one last thing I wanted to do today. We called Nancy to see if it was okay to visit Joe, my recipient, one last time. To my surprise, Nancy said, "Yes, but you'd better come over soon because Joe is going home today." We were amazed, as we expected Joe to be in the hospital significantly longer. We ran over right away. I pushed myself to make the walk from the hospital door to Joe's room without a wheel chair, which felt like a long journey. And there we found that same smiling man sitting in the chair, looking pretty great.

Joe told me how much he and his children have enjoyed reading my blog. And he said he wanted to apologize if he disappointed me when I had asked him how he was going to be putting my liver to good use, as his list focused on his family and not on, as he said, "climbing Mount Kilimanjaro." He just doesn't have that kind of bucket list, he explained.

I responded to Joe that he hadn't disappointed me and that I'd had the chance to reflect a bit regarding my own father. "My father is now 78," I told Joe, "and I think back on all the things that he has been able to experience with his family in the past nine years. Becoming a great-grandfather. Seeing the achievements of his grandchildren. Experiencing the Eagles winning the Super Bowl. And the times that he has been there for me when I've needed him most."

"I'm so grateful," I told Joe, "that I'm able to give you the same opportunities."

Carol and I hugged Joe and Nancy, and we said goodbye, knowing that last Friday we became connected through a liver, but now we're also connected through a heart.

The Meaning of Living
July 15, 2019

Today marks 10 days since my liver donation surgery,
and I've been amazed with my rate of recovery.

We returned to Connecticut on Saturday. I took my
dream team - Carol and my dad - for a thank-you
dinner at Bird Man Juke Joint, my favorite new local
restaurant. I've started responding to work emails
and started to make some work phone calls. I
reunited with my band and sang a few songs at
rehearsal. And today I took a two-mile walk and felt
great.

All of these things leave me feeling absolutely
exhausted, and I see all of them as part of my
returning to physical, and - just as importantly –
spiritual, normalcy.

A few weeks before my surgery, a friend sent me a
link to a segment from the film, *Monty Python's The
Meaning of Life*, focused on live organ transplants. It's
definitely not a sketch for the squeamish and, while
some might find it funny, it certainly doesn't reflect
my actual experience nor answer any great questions
about our existence.

In the days since my operation, however, I have found
it important to think about the meaning of what just
happened, among other things - and this might sound
crazy - because after being so focused on donating my
liver for over a year and a half, I wanted to avoid any
kind of post-surgery depression, a realization that

such a sense of personal purpose no longer stands in front of me.

Someone pointed out to me recently that the organ I was donating is called the "liver." And while I don't think this experience has given me a special insight into the meaning of life - the powerful question of why we were created, it has given me cause to think about the meaning of living, or at least *my* meaning of living.

In that regard, I'd like to share the following, after which I anticipate my postings to this blog to become much less frequent (barring any major developments).

For me, the meaning of living includes striving to be my best self; honoring my loved ones; soaking up the experiences that our world has to offer; building a better world; and inspiring others. In looking back at the past 10 days and the past year and a half, through those lenses, I have the following reflections.

STRIVING TO BE MY BEST SELF: While one of my key drivers in deciding to donate my liver was to strive to be my best self, I must acknowledge that I'm having a reckoning with the notion of altruism. While I entered into a process to save the life of someone I didn't know, I'm not sure I would properly describe my action as being entirely selfless, as certainly I was driven by the sense of accomplishment and good I would feel by having such an impact on someone else's life. And I'm not sure that matters. At the same time, this long odyssey inspired me to be my best self in so many other ways, including getting and keeping myself in the best possible physical condition leading up to the surgery (which has certainly had a major effect on my recovery). That's included not having a drink of alcohol since the beginning of 2018. Several people have asked me if I will resume any alcohol consumption or, at least, make a toast to my completed liver donation. While I'm uncertain on that front, I'm leaning towards "no." I don't feel like I've missed out on anything by not drinking, and I don't believe I've ever had a life experience that was improved because of alcohol. Most important, I think it's vital for me to remember, going forward, that being my best self doesn't require life-risking procedures as much as it involves an everyday commitment to wake up determined to make the right choices for myself and for others, driven by a sense of values and purpose.

HONORING MY LOVED ONES: I made the choice to donate my liver in order to pay tribute to my late mother, and I was so honored to have my father, daughters, son-in-law, and Carol there in Pittsburgh and to see their obvious pride for what I did. And it became clearer and clearer to me in the past week how I failed to properly take into account the stress and worry that I caused my loved ones, in particular, my dream team of Carol and my father. This was a huge surgery with a significant recovery, and while I was the one with the soreness and fatigue, I think the greater burden was placed on them, sitting by my bedside, taking care of me, and worrying. It wasn't until we were meeting my recipient, Joe, and he asked my father what he thought about my decision, that I understood just how much I had worried him. I am, by nature, an adventurer and a risk-taker, and I realize I need to be more cognizant of the concerns of those I love. And so, while I may choose to jump out of an airplane next year (which my father has done twice), I'm not planning to follow up my liver donation with a kidney donation in the near future, unless that donation is to save someone I love.

SOAKING UP THE EXPERIENCES THAT OUR WORLD HAS TO OFFER: While I haven't owned up to this until recently, one of the reasons I chose to donate my liver was to be a pioneer. When I travel, I love to go to places that I don't know many people who have traveled to before; and, while I have a friend who donated his kidney (and inspired me in this process), donating my liver felt like uncharted territory. In fact, although when I asked Joe what he wanted to do with his new liver, he told me that he didn't have a bucket list, he enabled me to check a box on my bucket list by receiving my donation. Part of my meaning of living will always include soaking up the beauty of our world - especially adventurous travel, beautiful music and theatre, and incredible food. I'll be thinking about what's next on my list and to what extent I can combine those experiences with opportunities to make positive impact. Until my surgery was scheduled for July, I had designs on visiting Uganda this fall, both to see gorillas and to find a way to make some difference there. That's going to wait for a bit, as I want to make sure I'm fully healthy before that kind of travel; but there's so much to soak up in this world and I want my sponge to be continually saturated.

BUILDING A BETTER WORLD: On that fateful night of December 8, 2017, when I made the decision to donate my liver, the question that I started with was how I could make a meaningful impact on the world in honor of my 50th birthday. For me, the answer that I came to was to directly save one person's life, something that I've never had the opportunity to do before. And there are so many ways that so many people work on a daily basis to build a better world, whether giving of their time, giving of their pocketbooks, or giving of their lives. I have wonderful friends who have adopted multiple foster children. I have friends who advocate for people in need. And in my professional life, every day I work with those who generously give time and money to save the lives of people they will never meet. While I don't know all the things that I'll look to do next, one idea that resonates very strongly with me is to see if I can fix the problem of there being no national database for liver donation. It was frustrating that I had to wait so long and work so hard to find my match, and I wouldn't want others to be discouraged from the process because it isn't as easy as it should be. And I want to confess that, while I went into this process feeling it would be okay if I didn't meet my recipient, it feels particularly rewarding to know the impact that I've had on Joe and his family. I'm guided by a great lyric written by my friend, Mark Erelli: *"So I'll sing of love and truth and try to practice what I preach; and if I can't change the world I'll change the world within my reach. And what better place to start than here and now with me and you? We are only passing through."*

INSPIRING OTHERS: Of those things that I've experienced through this process - aspiring to be my best self, honoring my mother, having an extraordinary journey, and build a better world for someone in need - the opportunity to inspire others is one that needn't end with my surgery, and I won't let it end there. It's the reason why I don't feel a sense of post-surgery depression. It's why I've tried to be as transparent as possible throughout my process. And it's why I've written this blog. Despite some of my internal conflicts noted above, knowing what I know now, I would absolutely make the same choice in being a living liver donor. I found the process to be extraordinarily rewarding in countless ways. And, while my experience may not be the same as everyone else's, the pain and discomfort I felt after my surgery were so much less than I would have imagined. Knowing that liver donation isn't the right thing for everyone for a whole wealth of reasons, there are so many for whom it could be a life-changing (and indeed a life-saving) choice. I want to continue sharing my experience, in the hope that I might be able to inspire others to do the same (or to seek out other ways in which they might save lives). In that regard, I would be happy, honored, and fulfilled to have the opportunity to speak to groups, write articles, and have one-on-one conversations about the living liver donation process. I'm here to answer questions for potential donors and would relish the chance to speak in any kind of venue. I want to be a poster boy, an advocate, and an information-provider. In that way, my experience and its impact needn't end.

As I noted above, I'm not sure what's going to happen with this blog from this point forward. I may post infrequently. It may go dormant. And so I want to say thank you to those of you who have followed my story and who have shared it with others. It has been a richer journey to have you along with me.

Perhaps I'll have a new revelation one night that will begin a new adventure and tale to tell. But as I finish writing this entry, I'm eternally thankful for a decision I made on December 8, 2017, those countless people who supported me in so many ways throughout my process, and those of you who have taken an interest in my story. Indeed, David's Chopped Liver is now a part of Joe, and I couldn't be more grateful.

One Minus Two-Thirds Equals Almost Two
October 3, 2019

It's October 30, nearly four months since my liver transplant surgery, and today I find myself at UPMC in Pittsburgh, the place where this profound and powerful experience took place.

It has been an amazing day, with some of the amazement simply being in returning to UPMC and reconnecting with this place and its wonderful people in a fully lucid state.

I've been feeling great. I've told many people recently that, if I didn't have a scar, you could convince me that I never had the surgery. And while some of that is because of how perfect I have been feeling physically, I must acknowledge that the other part is, in looking back, much of my time here in July is now a bit of a blur. While the medication was great - and at times spectacular - it also clouded my memory a bit. In fact, I'm grateful that I've been writing this blog not only for you, but also for me, as I've had the opportunity in reading it to go back and relive the experience (at least as I perceived it then).

While I came here today for my four-month follow-up appointment, I knew that a highlight would be meeting with my recipient, Joe, and his wife, Nancy. We met for breakfast at the hospital, and I was delighted that they brought along their five-year-old grandson, Eli - in particular because I know that spending time with Eli was one of those things Joe really wanted to live for.

Joe is doing great and looks fantastic. He told me that I gave him a really good liver. He's been going for regular follow-up appointments and testing, for which the frequency has just been reduced, and he'll be on anti-rejection medicine for the rest of his life (which he said is no big deal whatsoever), but he's back to his full level of activity. He's biking, and he's trap shooting (he said the first time he shot, it hurt, but he very quickly got used to it), and he's enjoying his family. He said his liver tests are all in perfect ranges, and he believes his liver is close to 100% in size now. I really couldn't be happier about the person who received my liver and about his recovery.

And it's remarkable how people can become friends simply because they share an organ of the same origin. I would never have met Joe and Nancy without our connection through transplant, and now I can only assume we'll have a friendship for the rest of our lives.

I'll say it once again. While Joe may be eternally grateful for what I've given him, I feel equally grateful for what he gave me: the opportunity to fulfill my dream of being a living liver donor. It's a true gift.

After meeting with Joe, I wanted to return to 11-North, the wing of the hospital in which I spent the bulk of my recovery. I was surprised and grateful to be recognized by some of the staff and to have the opportunity to reunite with Alison Cole, my favorite nurse. I was happy to be able to give her a hug and thank her for the great care she took of me. It felt surreal to step back into that space again, but perhaps no more surreal than it felt to be there the first time.

This afternoon was the medical part of the day, starting with my CT scan. For all my nervousness (again) about whether I'd be going into a tube, it turned out to be an open machine that I went into feet first. The process couldn't have been easier. There was even a beautiful photo of the sky on the ceiling of the room to provide a sense of calm, and the machine lit up with a smiley face as it moved you inside.

Following a quick lunch in the hospital cafeteria, I was off to the transplant center to meet with my surgeon, Dr. Humar. I was happy, while sitting in the examination room, to see Elaine Lander, my Living Donor Coordinator, come into the room. Elaine has been my primary point of contact since the day my process began at UPMC.

And then in came Dr. Humar, one of my great heroes. He asked me how I was feeling, and I told him that I couldn't be better. He pulled up the images from my CT scan. While I had been previously told that my liver would be fully grown back (from the 36% I was left with after surgery) in about 60 days, Dr. Humar told me that it's a slower process than that. The image of my liver looked to be about 80%, he thought. (A friend has been asking me how my liver knows when to stop growing. I asked Dr. Humar, and he said it's just the incredible way our body is programmed. It just knows when to stop.) More importantly, however, he told me that my liver looked healthy and that there was no fluid around it that would be cause for concern. He looked at the results of my blood tests from a couple of months ago and said that all my liver levels looked to be in perfect order. He looked at my scar and was happy with the way I've been healing.

He said goodbye and that he hopes to see me again; and, after the lab drew a few more tubes of blood to test later today, I was sent on my way.

I knew I'd have to come back here for follow-up testing. I didn't know how gratified I'd feel to step back into this building and reunite with these people.

Who knows when or if I'll see some of them again? I hope I will. Joe, Nancy, and I already have tentative plans to meet next summer.

Joe and I. We share an organ of common origin. And, after nearly four months, one minus two-thirds equals almost two.

I Still Hate Needles
April 29, 2020

Today is one day short of six months since I was in
Pittsburgh for my first follow-up appointment for my
liver donation surgery.

A number of things have changed since then.

In late 2019, Carol and I realized that what each of us
was looking for in a relationship was different, and
we decided to transition to being friends. Indeed, she
remains one of my best friends and confidantes; and,
most importantly, she will always be one of the heroes
of this story. I could not have done it without her, and
for that, I will be forever grateful.

I have also joined the board of Donate Life CT, and
I've been in conversation with the American Liver
Foundation, all in hopes that I can encourage more
people to become organ donors and, ultimately,
realize my goal of creating infrastructure that makes
it easier for prospective altruistic donors to find their
matches.

I've continued to be periodically in touch with Joe and
Nancy, and Joe continues to do well.

And I must admit that I've begun to have a hankering
(yes, it feels like a very strange word in this situation)
to donate something else. My sense has been that the
only other option would be a kidney, but I know it's
too soon for that and it would be too much to put my
family (and my body) through again right now.

I've also been thinking about how I might craft an ending to the story of my liver donation journey, and I figured that would come with my being honored at the Donate Life CT annual gala (an incredibly kind and unnecessary gesture which was scheduled for March 13) or with my one-year check-up at UPMC, which is scheduled for May 20 in Pittsburgh (actually about six weeks before the one-year anniversary of my surgery).

And then, early this year, the whole world changed - not just for me, but for everyone - as the COVID-19 virus emerged and engulfed the planet. The Donate Life gala was cancelled and won't be held until the fall of 2021. And I can't imagine that I'm getting on a plane next month to fly to Pittsburgh. That appointment will inevitably be transitioned to a video conference.

A little over a month ago, on March 25, I found myself waiting in a two-hour-long car line in New Rochelle, New York, with my new significant other, waiting for her to be tested for the coronavirus. I had called 911 a couple of days earlier when she had developed a fever and was feeling some chest tightness, and it triggered her eligibility to get tested. I had no qualms about being in the car with her. It was clear to me that I already had the virus too. I was told that I would have to wait until she had tested positive in order for me to qualify for the test. But when we finally reached the front of the line, the soldier doing the intake asked, "Does he want to get tested too?" Of course, I said "yes," and by the next evening, it was confirmed that we were both COVID-19 positive.

While I was writing every day during my COVID-19 experience, I'm not going to share all of that with you. Indeed, my story won't be such a rare story when it comes to coronavirus, and there will undoubtedly be countless books written on the topic. My battle with COVID-19 was more than mild and less than severe. There were a couple of days that I thought it was inevitable that I would end up in the hospital, but thankfully, that didn't happen. My symptoms - fever, chills, night sweats, cough, sore throat - passed in about ten days, followed by two weeks of debilitating fatigue. I'm grateful to be on the other side of it.

And having had and recovered from COVID-19 opened up an opportunity to - at least for the moment - address the urgings that I have been feeling.

So, even though my greatest fear when it came to my liver transplant surgery was about needles and blood (along with MRIs), I found myself last evening at the New York Blood Center with a needle in my arm, volunteering to be a convalescent plasma donor, in the hope that I've developed antibodies that can help others who are more severely affected than I was to fight the disease.

While I've donated two-thirds of a major organ, I'd never donated blood before. I can understand why this seems crazy, but I have more fear about giving blood than I did about giving my liver.

And I had tried and failed to do so for the first time last week. I was unaware that I needed to drink a ton of water during the day, and my blood simply wasn't flowing enough for a donation. I felt defeated. The technicians had really tried, in both arms, digging around for a vein so much in my left arm that, when I went for my second appointment last night, I was still bruised and clearly had a hematoma.

But I still went last evening, cutting out a little early from a Donate Life Zoom board meeting, having drunk what felt like an entire water tower, and ready to present my right arm as a single target for Tara, the newest contestant at "Find David's Vein."

To my great delight (and pride that I was no longer a plasma-donor failure), Tara hit the mark.

As I lay back in the chair for an hour, having 800 mL of plasma drawn, the man giving blood next to me was studying Talmud, and I thought back to that sign I saw on my first trip to UPMC just over a year ago, quoting the Talmud that: "Whoever saves one life, it is as if he saved an entire world."

Trying to distract myself from the amount of time left to go, I spoke with Tara and some of the other technicians about my liver donation, scrolling on my phone with my one available hand to show them the photo that Dr. Humar had taken of what was left of my liver, after he had removed the larger part to be implanted into Joe. They were fascinated.

I asked Tara what would happen with my plasma, and she told me that, after it was tested for any infectious diseases, it would go right to the hospital and be given to a COVID-19 patient or two who were waiting for it. I couldn't help but smile.

I'm scheduled to go back to the blood center to donate again next week. And I'll probably go one more time the week after.

There are lives to be saved, and it seems a much simpler way than last time that I can make a difference.

And I'll continue to turn my head the other way.

I still hate needles.